WASHINGTON WIZARDS

ALL-TIME GREATS

BY LUKE HANLON

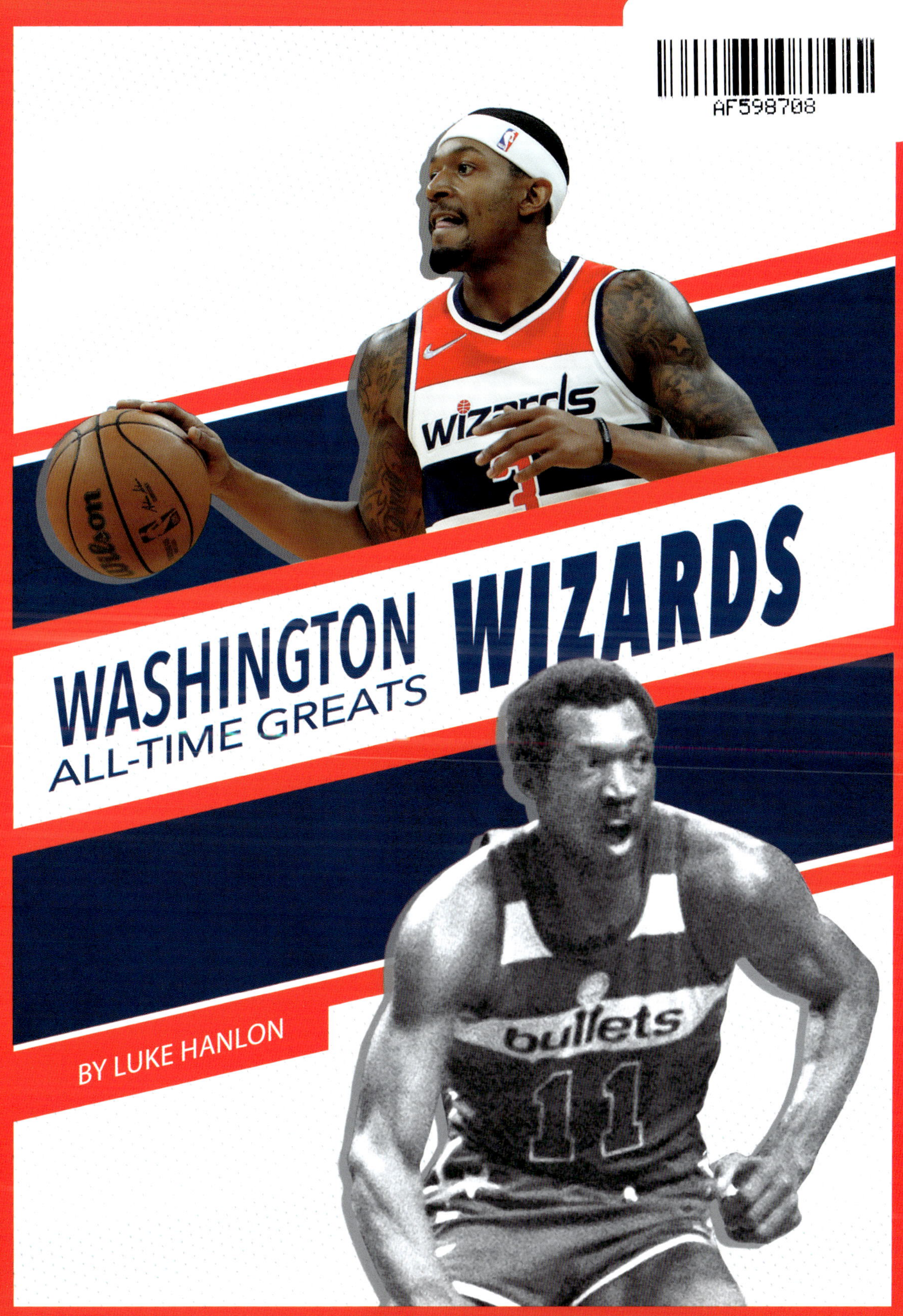

Book design by Jake Slavik
Cover design by Jake Slavik

Photographs ©: Scott Audette/AP Images, cover (top), 1 (top); AP Images, cover (bottom), 1 (bottom), 7, 8, 10; Paul Cannon/AP Images, 4; Richard Drew/AP Images, 12; Ted Mathias/AP Images, 15; Manuel Balce Ceneta/AP Images, 16; Kirby Lee/AP Images, 19; Alex Brandon/AP Images, 20

Press Box Books, an imprint of Press Room Editions.

ISBN
978-1-63494-669-8 (library bound)
978-1-63494-693-3 (paperback)
978-1-63494-740-4 (epub)
978-1-63494-717-6 (hosted ebook)

Library of Congress Control Number: 2022919254

Distributed by North Star Editions, Inc.
2297 Waters Drive
Mendota Heights, MN 55120
www.northstareditions.com

Printed in the United States of America
082023

ABOUT THE AUTHOR

Luke Hanlon is a sportswriter and editor based in Minneapolis.

TABLE OF CONTENTS

BELLAMY
8

CHAPTER 1

GETTING TO WASHINGTON

The Washington Wizards were introduced to the NBA in 1961–62. However, the team was known as the Chicago Packers then. The Packers had the top pick in the NBA Draft before their first season. They used it on center **Walt Bellamy**. The 6'11" big man dominated near the basket. That's how he averaged

STAT SPOTLIGHT

POINTS PER GAME IN A SEASON

WIZARDS TEAM RECORD

Walt Bellamy: 31.6 (1961-62)

27.6 points and 16.6 rebounds per game in just over four seasons with the team.

Before the 1963–64 season, the team moved to Baltimore and changed their name to the Bullets. Forward **Gus Johnson** joined Bellamy for the first season in Baltimore. By 1964–65, both Bellamy and Johnson were All-Stars. That duo also led the Bullets to the playoffs for the first time that season.

The Bullets drafted another superstar in 1967. They selected guard **Earl Monroe** with the second overall pick. "The Pearl" dazzled fans with his flashy play style. And he used his skill set to score in bunches. Monroe paired nicely with **Wes Unseld**. The 6'7" center was taken second overall a year after Monroe. They each won the Rookie of the Year award. Unseld was an elite rebounder. And he had a

bullets
41
bullets
UNSELD
41

knack for tossing perfect outlet passes to start fast breaks.

Monroe and Unseld led the Bullets to the NBA Finals in 1971. However, they were

RARE COMPANY

Wes Unseld won more than just the Rookie of the Year in 1968–69. His averages of 13.8 points and 18.2 rebounds per game helped him earn the Most Valuable Player (MVP) Award as well. He was only the second player in league history to be the MVP as a rookie. NBA legend Wilt Chamberlain did it in 1959–60.

swept in four games by the Milwaukee Bucks. Monroe left after one more season. But another future Hall of Fame big man soon joined to partner with Unseld. The Bullets traded for **Elvin Hayes** in 1972. The dominant forward played nine seasons for the Bullets. He and Unseld were the stars of the team when it moved to Landover, Maryland, in 1973. The team now represented the Washington, DC, area as the Washington Bullets. The two stars led the Bullets to three Finals appearances between 1975 and 1979. The team won its first title in 1978.

56
BOSTON
29
CELTICS
CELTICS
BALLARD
42

CHAPTER 2

WIZARDRY

Wes Unseld and Elvin Hayes were gone by the 1981–82 season. However, it wasn't long before other players stepped up. Small forward **Greg Ballard** hadn't played much in the 1978 NBA Finals. But he developed into a reliable scorer. His 18.8 points per game led the Bullets in their first season without Unseld and Hayes.

Jeff Ruland took over as the team's main scorer in 1982–83. The 6'10" center was a double-double machine. That skill helped

BOL
10

him earn him two All-Star appearances while with Washington.

Jeff Malone was also a two-time All-Star with the Bullets. The shooting guard averaged more than 20 points per game for five straight years with the team. After seven seasons with Washington, he departed as the team's second all-time leading scorer in 1990.

Holding down the defense was 7'7" **Manute Bol**. The South Sudanese center didn't score much. But he led the NBA in blocks as a rookie in 1985–86 with 5.0 per game. **Bernard King** was a secondary scorer behind Malone for three seasons. Once Malone

STAT SPOTLIGHT

BLOCKS IN A GAME

WIZARDS TEAM RECORD

Manute Bol: 15 (Feb. 26, 1987 & Jan. 25, 1986)

was gone, King really showed off his scoring. The forward averaged 28.4 points per game in 1990–91.

However, Washington continued to pile up losing seasons in the early 1990s. Then they got two talented forwards in 1994. The team traded for **Chris Webber**. And Washington selected **Juwan Howard** fifth overall in the draft. The 21-year-olds had played together at the University of Michigan. They both showcased great scoring and rebounding skills to become All-Stars in

BECOMING THE WIZARDS

The prime minister of Israel, Yitzhak Rabin, was killed by gun violence in 1995. He was a good friend of Wizards' owner Abe Pollin. After this, Pollin no longer wanted Washington's team name to be Bullets. A fan vote held in 1997 led to the name Wizards. The team also changed its colors from red, white, and blue to white, blue, and bronze.

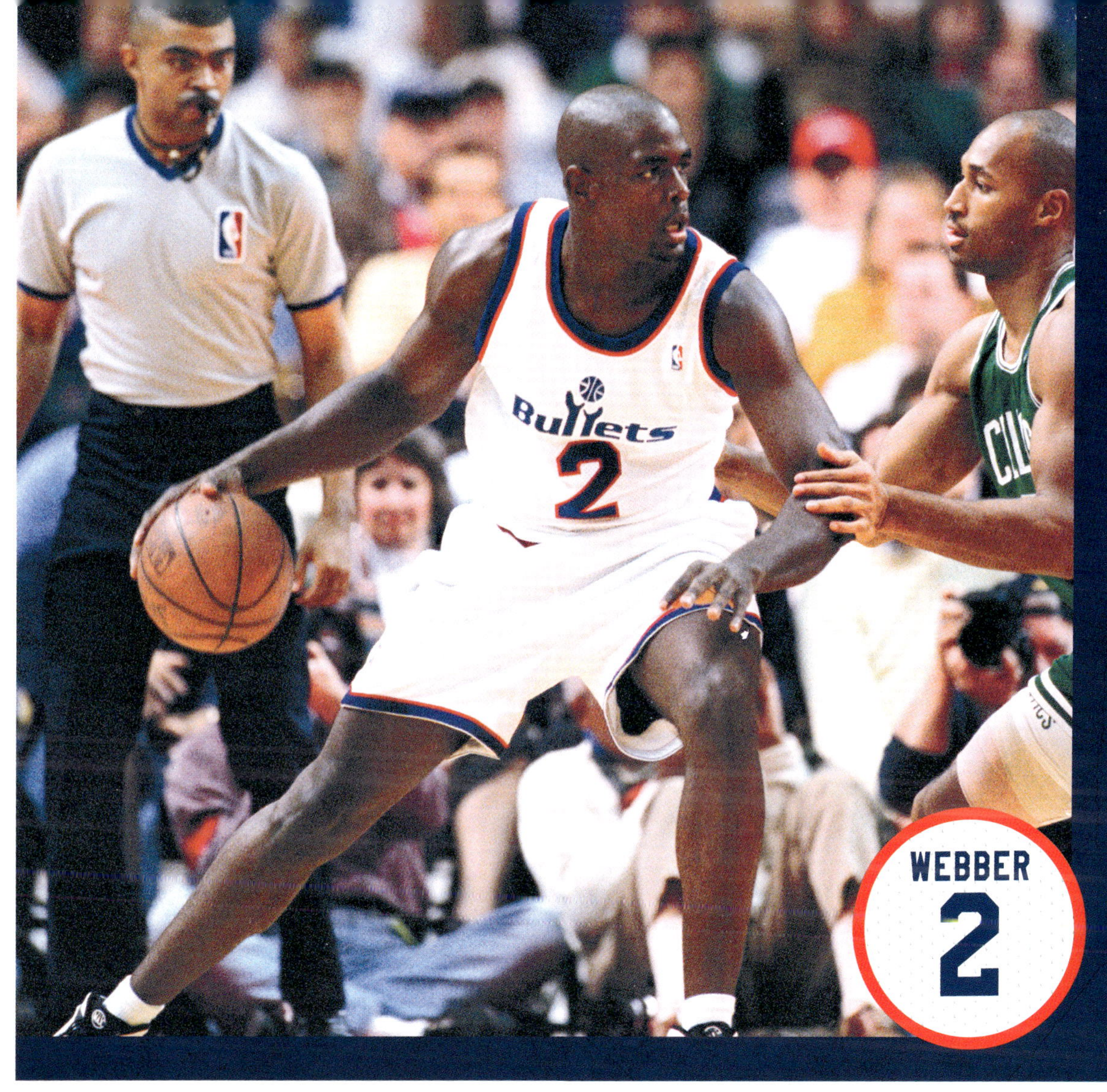

Washington. Webber and Howard were still the stars of the team when Washington changed nicknames. The Bullets became the Wizards in 1997–98.

ARENAS
0

CHAPTER 3

MODERN WIZARDS

The Wizards missed the playoffs for seven straight seasons after the name change. Chris Webber was traded to the Sacramento Kings in 1998. And Juwan Howard was gone by 2001. Point guard **Gilbert Arenas** helped end that streak in 2005. "Agent Zero" could score from anywhere. He sometimes shot the ball far beyond the three-point line. Arenas's hot shooting led to three seasons of scoring more than 25 points per game for Washington.

The Wizards had two other talented players fill out the roster in the mid-2000s. Swingman

Larry Hughes was a solid two-way player. He thrived on defense. Hughes averaged an NBA-best 2.9 steals per game in 2004–05.

The secondary scorer helping Arenas was **Antawn Jamison**. The 6'8" forward was too big for smaller defenders. And he was too quick for bigger defenders. One of Jamison's best qualities was his leadership. He was the team captain at the time.

That core was gone by 2010. However, Washington added two game-changing

JORDAN THE WIZARD

After winning his sixth NBA championship with the Chicago Bulls in 1998, Michael Jordan retired from basketball. In 2000, he joined the Wizards' front office. He shocked the NBA when he added himself to the Wizards' roster for the 2001–02 season. "Air Jordan" played two seasons with the Wizards. He made the All-Star team both years.

WIZARDS
20
WIZARDS
0
Clippers
36
HUGHES
20

guards not long after. The team selected **John Wall** with the first pick in the 2010 draft. Wall was one of the quickest players in the NBA. He used that speed to get to the basket constantly.

And he always found open teammates. Wall averaged more than nine assists per game with Washington.

The Wizards added **Bradley Beal** with the third pick in 2012. While Wall ran the offense, Beal provided scoring. The guard could score from anywhere. But he was best at shooting threes. Wall and Beal combined to make seven All-Star games for Washington before Wall was traded in 2020.

Beal stuck around and was an All-Star again in 2021. Then he signed a long-term contract with the team in 2022. The Wizards hoped he would bring them back to the NBA Finals.

STAT SPOTLIGHT

CAREER ASSISTS

WIZARDS TEAM RECORD

John Wall: 5,282

TIMELINE

1961
WALT BELLAMY
(1961-65)
GUS JOHNSON
(1963-72)
EARL MONROE
(1967-71)
1970
WES UNSELD
(1968-81)
ELVIN HAYES
(1972-81)
GREG BALLARD
(1977-85)
1980
JEFF RULAND
(1981-86)
JEFF MALONE
(1983-90)
MANUTE BOL
(1985-88,
1993-94)
BERNARD KING
(1987-91)
1990
CHRIS WEBBER
(1994-98)
JUWAN HOWARD
(1994-2001)
2000
LARRY HUGHES
(2002-05)
GILBERT ARENAS
(2003-10)
ANTAWN JAMISON
(2004-10)
2010
JOHN WALL
(2010-20)
BRADLEY BEAL
(2012-)
2020
2023

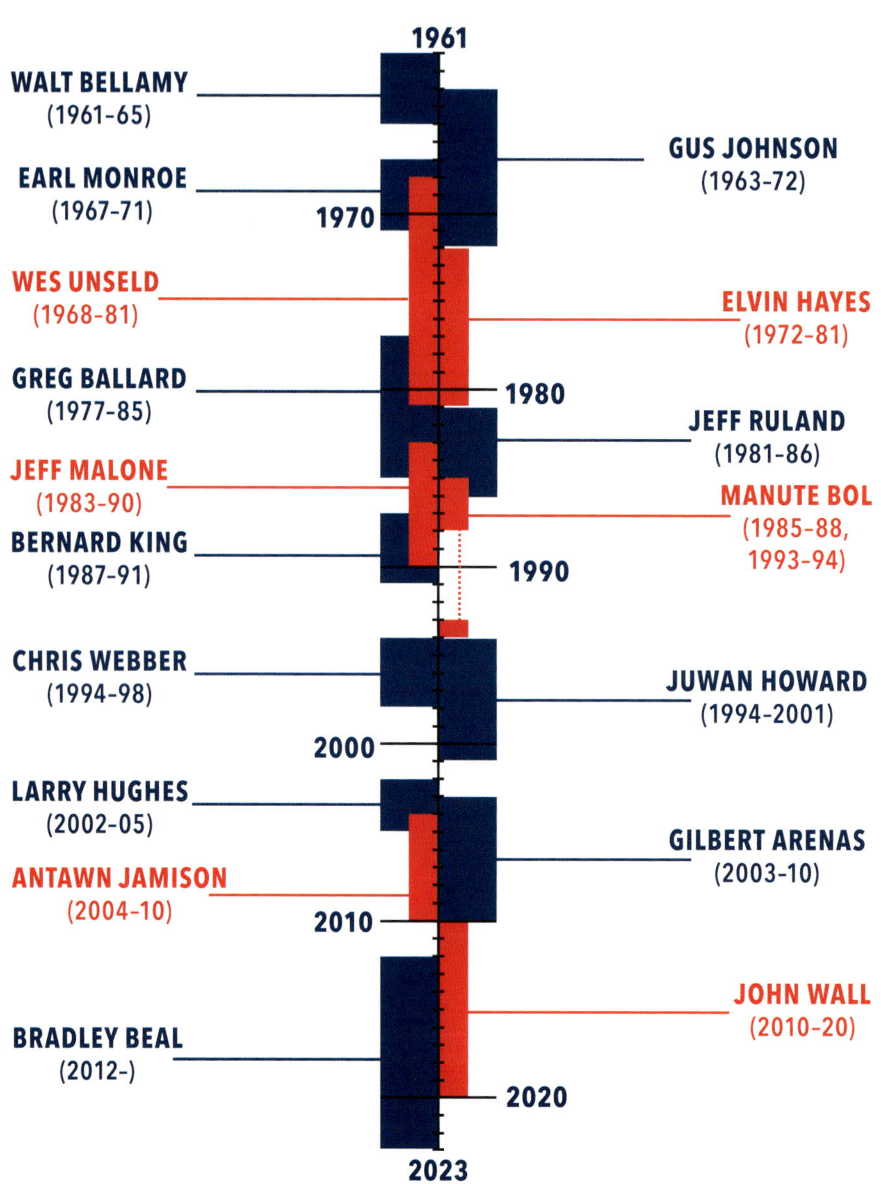

TEAM FACTS

WASHINGTON WIZARDS

Formerly: Chicago Packers (1961–62); Chicago Zephyrs (1962–63); Baltimore Bullets (1963–73); Capital Bullets (1973–74); Washington Bullets (1974–97)

First season: 1961–62

NBA championships: 1*

Key coaches:

Dick Motta (1976–77 to 1979–80) 185–143, 27–24 playoffs, 1 NBA title

Gene Shue (1966–67 to 1972–73, 1980–81 to 1985–86) 522–505, 19–36 playoffs

MORE INFORMATION

To learn more about the Washington Wizards, go to **pressboxbooks.com/AllAccess.**

These links are routinely monitored and updated to provide the most current information available.

Through 2021–22 season

GLOSSARY

contract
A written agreement that keeps a player with a team for a certain amount of time.

double-double
When a player reaches 10 or more of two different statistics in one game.

draft
An event that allows teams to choose new players coming into the league.

elite
The best of the best.

fast break
A play in which a team advances the ball up the floor quickly.

outlet pass
A pass made by a player after a rebound to start a fast break.

rookie
A first-year player.

swingman
A player who can play both guard and forward.

INDEX